INDIAN

Simple and Delicious

INDIAN

Ajoy Joshi

APPLE

Contents

A Word from Ajoy

As a young boy growing up in India in the early 1960s, I dreamt of eating in the Taj Mahal Hotel restaurants, famous for their masala dosai. Passing one on my way to school was the beginning of my love not only for masala dosai but for food in general. After I finished my schooling many paths were open to me, but I decided that I had to do something different. Hence I began the challenging but rewarding journey to become a cook. During my catering school days in Madras I was fortunate to work at the Taj Coramandel and Fisherman's Cove Hotels, the former as a waiter (providing the tips that sustained me financially) and the latter as a trainee cook (giving me the tips I needed to become a chef). The next step was very clear—I had to become an executive chef.

Working at the Taj Group of hotels, especially in the banquet kitchen as a sous-chef, was always exciting. Once the food was cooked, it was displayed attractively, which brought out my artistic instincts. After hard work, and more hard work, I realized my dream in 1988, when I was appointed executive chef of the Gateway Hotel in Bangalore. This also opened up opportunities for me to explore other parts of the world and take my cooking skills offshore.

Sixteen years and six restaurants later, I am at Nilgiri's in Sydney, discovering my roots and cooking Indian food with a simple philosophy guided by the famous Hyderabadi saying that good food comes with fursat (leisure) and mohabbat (love). The food at Nilgiri's is simple, and the menu small, which allows the chefs to focus on the finer details of each dish.

Cooking Indian food, like any other great cuisine, is a celebration of life. These recipes are a selection of some of my most popular dishes, presented in a format that makes them easy to prepare. I hope that you enjoy the journey of cooking each dish as much as the pleasure of eating it. For more recipes and information about Indian food, see my book *Indian Home Cooking*.

Finally, as any self-respecting Indian would say at the conclusion of a good meal, "Anha datha sukhi bhava"—"May the provider of this food be happy and content."

Culinary Traditions

The cuisine of India, in its variety, sights, textures, aromas and rituals, reflects the essence of the country in every way. In such a large country, with all manner of climates, each region has its own ingredients that can be grown or harvested readily. The west coast is especially renowned for its tantalizing seafood dishes, such as Meen Kozhambu and Shrimp Reiachado. In southern cuisine, coconut, curry leaves and mustard seeds, tropical fruits, tamarind, fresh and dried chili peppers and rice-based dishes are all important. In the north and heart of the country, the food is not as heavily spiced or fiery as it is in the south. Ghee, Indian clarified butter, is commonly used, and the Punjab is where tandoori cooking, in which meat, chicken and bread are cooked in a clay oven, began. Wonderful flat breads such as chappati are famous in the north.

More than 80 percent of India's population are Hindu, with many following vegetarianism and the majority avoiding beef, and vegetables are an important part of every meal in every region. The choice of vegetable depends on the season and the other foods on the menu. For example, a green vegetable is always offered with a red meat dish. In a vegetarian meal, one would expect to be served a vegetable, one or two lentil-based dishes, perhaps a dish featuring paneer (homemade cheese) and rice and/or bread, along with accompaniments such as chutney and a yogurt-based raita.

Indians generally keep in mind principles of Ayurveda, an ancient philosophy of health and healing that is still strong today and has gained popularity in Western countries. Foods and spices are combined not only for their taste but also for their healing properties. The foundation of every meal—rice or bread, lentils, and oil and/or ghee—provides the three major essential nutrients of carbohydrates, protein and fat. The addition of spices and herbs contributes certain medicinal benefits according to Ayurvedic principles. For example, ground turmeric is a powerful natural antioxidant and anti-inflammatory agent.

The attention paid to serving fresh vegetables along with pickles and yogurt-based dishes also helps to ensure a balanced diet by providing a range of vitamins and minerals. The pickles and yogurt are said to aid digestion. Much

consideration is given to the elements of a meal: salt, bitter/sour and hot/pungent being three of the most important. According to the Ayurvedic philosophy, these must appear in every meal, though not necessarily in every dish, to create a balance. Pickles and chutneys, the intensely seasoned condiments served at an Indian meal, help balance a meal by providing any key tastes not already present. Just one or two condiments are served at a meal, and diners mix a little with the other foods. These condiments also act as appetite stimulants and digestive aids.

During their rule in India, the British brought tea plants from China to India and began establishing massive tea plantations. It wasn't long before Indians themselves enthusiastically took up the beverage, adding spices such as cardamom, cinnamon, cloves, anise, pepper, ginger and fennel to create the fragrant and sweet masala chai, meaning spiced tea. Chai is to the Indians what good espresso is to the Italians. India is now the major producer of tea in the world. The yogurt-based drinks called lassi are usually served only at breakfast and provide a nutritious start to the day.

NOTE Unlike the Anglo-Indian food served by many restaurants outside India, the recipes in this book are authentic ethnic Indian food as prepared in many Indian homes. For a traditional Indian meal, start with one of the snacks or appetizers then serve several dishes at once as the main part of the meal, followed by dessert. Most of the recipes in this book will form part of a meal that serves eight to ten.

Ingredients and Spices

AJWAIN These tiny seeds have the flavor of thyme, with peppery overtones, and are similar in appearance to celery seeds.

ASAFOETIDA Made from the dried gum of a giant fennel plant, this yellow powder's foul aroma disappears when it is added to food, leaving a mild onion or garlic flavor. It also helps prevent the gastric distress associated with eating lentils and beans.

CARDAMOM Whole green cardamom pods are filled with fragrant, tiny black seeds and are a key ingredient in spice mixes, sweet and savory dishes. For best flavor, grind your own just before using. You can also buy pre-ground cardamom seeds. Brown (also called black) cardamom pods yield tiny, smoky-flavored seeds. The pods are used in savory dishes and are a vital ingredient in many meat dishes.

CHAT MASALA Sometimes called chaat masala, this tasty, tart mixture of toasted and ground spices and other ingredients is sprinkled over food before serving. It may contain any of the following: black salt, table salt, asafoetida, cumin, coriander, dried mint, ginger, mace, garam masala, pomegranate seeds, chili peppers, black pepper and amchur powder (ground dried green mango).

CHICKPEAS (GARBANZO BEANS), SPLIT Known as channa dal and gram lentils, these are smaller than those used in Western cuisines although the flavor is very similar. Yellow split peas may be substituted.

CHILI PEPPERS Chop fresh chilies very finely or grind to a paste in a small food processor. Use good-quality, whole dried serrano chilies unless specified otherwise. If you prefer less heat, deseed or decrease the number of chilies used.

CINNAMON STICKS Also called cinnamon quills, these hard sticks consist of rolled and layered pieces of bark from the cinnamon tree. Cassia, also a dried bark, has a more intense fragrance. Either can be used in these recipes.

CLOVES The dried buds of a tree that grows in Southeast Asia and the West Indies, cloves are a key ingredient in spice mixes. They also contribute a sharp sweetness to rice dishes, meat dishes and desserts.

CORIANDER SEEDS From the plant that provides cilantro (coriander), these are usually dry-roasted in a frying pan before being ground. Freshly ground coriander seeds have a fragrance that is both lemony and herbaceous.

CUMIN SEEDS These are the seeds from a plant in the parsley family. Briefly dry-roasting cumin seeds brings out their flavor, which is earthy, pungent and a little bitter. Used whole or ground, cumin seeds are a common ingredient in spice mixes, many savory dishes and raitas. Black cumin seeds have a slightly less bitter taste.

CURRY LEAVES Native to India and Sri Lanka, these dark green shiny, soft leaves, also known as karhi patta, have a strong savory flavor with a hint of citrus. Dried curry leaves may be substituted.

FENNEL SEEDS From the fennel plant, these are used whole or ground to add an aniseed-like flavor to meat dishes, vegetable dishes, desserts, pickles and chutneys. Whole fennel seeds, plain or sugar coated, are served at the end of a meal as a digestive aid.

FENUGREEK Whole or ground fenugreek seeds are used along with the dried leaves; the two forms are not interchangeable. The seeds, roasted to bring out their bitter, sharp and nutty flavor, are added to spice mixes, breads, chutneys and lentil dishes. Fenugreek leaves have a subtle sweetness.

FROM LEFT *Ajwain; cardamom pods; asafoetida.*

GARLIC AND GINGER To prepare for cooking, process in a food processor with enough vegetable oil to make a paste. Keep in an airtight container in the refrigerator for up to 3 days.

GHEE Also known as clarified butter, ghee is very rich. Using a mixture of vegetable oil and melted unsalted butter gives a less imposing flavor.

INDIAN BAY LEAVES Despite their name, Indian bay leaves come from the cassia tree. They are larger and have a slightly sweeter flavor than the European variety.

JAGGERY A sweetener made from dehydrated sugarcane juice. Dark brown sugar may be substituted.

LENTILS Black lentils (urad dal or black gram) are quite small compared with other lentils and cook more quickly. They are also ground into split black lentil flour (urad flour). Yellow split peas (matar dal) have a mild flavor, and when well cooked, a mushy texture. Green (brown) lentils are a little larger than other lentils, have a slightly nutty flavor and hold their shape when cooked.

MUSTARD SEEDS Brown or black mustard seeds are always crackled in hot oil for a few seconds to release their pungent flavor. Mustard oil is a popular cooking medium in India.

NUTMEG AND MACE The seed of a tree, nutmeg is ground and most commonly teamed with sweet foods though it is also an ingredient in some spice mixes for savory dishes. Its mild, sweet flavor complements white and red meats. Mace is red outer coating of nutmeg, and blade mace is the whole coating, which has been

FROM LEFT Fenugreek; turmeric; chat masala.

removed from the nutmeg and dried; it has a coarse, netted appearance. More pungent than nutmeg, mace enhances pulaos and seafood dishes.

PAPRIKA Sweet red bell peppers (capsicums) are dried and ground to produce this spice, which is used to flavor and add color to savory dishes.

RICE AND CHICKPEA FLOUR Medium to coarse rice flour is used in dosai, (fermented rice pancakes), finer flour is used in steamed rice cakes, batters and some desserts. Chickpea (garbanzo bean) flour is a fine yellow flour with a nutty taste, used in batters, pastries and doughs.

SAFFRON Dried stigmas from a variety of crocus flower, each of which produces only three stigmas, this is the most costly spice in the world. Saffron threads are generally soaked in a warm liquid to release their intense gold-yellow color and pungent, earthy aroma and taste.

STAR ANISE This spice is the dried star-shaped fruit from a variety of evergreen magnolia tree. Its flavor is similar to that of aniseed, but has more depth of flavor and sweetness.

TAMARIND CONCENTRATE Made from the pulp and seeds from the pods of the tamarind tree, this adds a tart, fruity tang to savory dishes. Unlike blocks of compressed tamarind pulp, it does not require any preparation.

TURMERIC This spice is used in most savory dishes to lend a deep gold color and sharp and sometimes slightly bitter flavor. Derived from the root of a tropical plant, turmeric is generally dried and then ground, though it is also used fresh.

FROM LEFT *Jaggery; mustard seeds; curry leaves.*

Basic Spice Mixes

Baffad masala

2 cups dried Kashmiri red chili peppers,
broken into small pieces
⅔ cup coriander seeds
3 cinnamon sticks, about 3 inches
(8 cm) long, broken into small pieces
2½ teaspoons black peppercorns
4 teaspoons whole cloves
2 teaspoons cumin seeds
2½ teaspoons ground turmeric

In a large saucepan, combine chili peppers, coriander, cinnamon, peppercorns, cloves and cumin. Place over low heat and dry-roast until just fragrant.

Place spices in an airtight jar and add turmeric. Shake to combine and store in the refrigerator for up to 6 months.

When ready to use baffad masala, grind to a powder in a spice grinder. Use in Lamb Cutlets Baffad (page 36).

NOTE Use regular dried red chili peppers if Kashmiri ones are not available.

Sambhar masala

1⅓ cups coriander seeds
1 cup dried red chili peppers, broken
into small pieces
2 teaspoons fenugreek seeds
1½ teaspoons black mustard seeds
1 tablespoon cumin seeds
½-inch (12-mm) piece cinnamon stick
⅓ cup (1¾ oz/55 g) unsweetened
dried (desiccated) shredded coconut
¼ cup firmly packed fresh curry leaves
1½ teaspoons powdered asafoetida

Heat a small saucepan over low heat. Separately dry-roast coriander, chili peppers, fenugreek, mustard, cumin and cinnamon until fragrant and only lightly colored. Place roasted spices in a bowl.

Toast coconut in pan, stirring constantly, until lightly browned. Add to spices. Dry-roast curry leaves, tossing often, until crisp. Add to spices with asafoetida. Mix well and let cool.

Place mixture in an airtight jar and store in the refrigerator for up to 6 months. Just before using sambhar masala, grind to a powder in a spice grinder. Use in Sambhar (page 54).

Reiachado masala

4 dried red chili peppers, broken into
   small pieces
4 teaspoons black peppercorns
1 teaspoon cumin seeds
½ cup (2 fl oz/60 ml) white vinegar
4 teaspoons crushed garlic
1½ teaspoons tamarind concentrate
½ teaspoon ground turmeric

In a spice grinder, grind chili
peppers, peppercorns and cumin
seeds (without roasting) to a powder.
   In a small bowl, combine vinegar,
garlic and tamarind. Stir in ground
spices and turmeric, and mix well.
   Set aside to stand for
10–20 minutes. Use in Shrimp
Reiachado (page 30).

Step-by-step Garam masala

1 cinnamon stick, about 4 inches
   (10 cm) long, broken into small
   pieces
4 teaspoons whole green cardamom
   pods
3 brown or black cardamom pods
4 teaspoons whole cloves
4 teaspoons mace pieces
4 teaspoons black peppercorns
4 teaspoons fennel seeds
3 Indian bay leaves, torn into quarters
1 teaspoon freshly grated nutmeg

1. Heat a small saucepan over low
heat. Separately dry-roast cinnamon,
cardamom, cloves, mace,
peppercorns, fennel seeds and bay
leaves until fragrant and only lightly
colored. Make sure heat is not too
intense, as spices must not overbrown
or burn.
2. As each spice is roasted, place in
a bowl. Allow roasted spices to cool.
Add nutmeg, mix thoroughly and
place in an airtight jar. Store in the
refrigerator for up to 1 year.
3. Just before using garam masala,
grind to a powder in a spice grinder.

Appetizers

Mixed vegetable pakoras

Makes about 28 pakoras
BATTER
2⅔ cups (14 oz/440 g) chickpea
  (garbanzo bean) flour
1 teaspoon whole ajwain seeds
½ teaspoon chili powder
salt to taste
4 teaspoons vegetable oil
about 1¼ cups (10 fl oz/300 ml) water

vegetable oil, for deep-frying
1 red bell pepper (capsicum), seeded
  and cut into ½-inch (12-mm) dice
1 medium desiree potato, peeled and
  cut into ½-inch (12-mm) dice
1 large red or yellow (brown) onion, cut
  into ½-inch (12-mm) dice
1 medium globe eggplant (aubergine),
  unpeeled, cut into ½-inch (12-mm)
  dice
Cucumber Raita (page 55) for serving

To make batter: In a bowl, combine flour, ajwain seeds, chili powder and salt. In a small saucepan, heat oil until it begins to smoke, then quickly stir into flour mixture. Add enough water to form a thick, smooth batter.

Fill a wok with vegetable oil to a depth of 3 inches (7.5 cm). Heat oil over medium–high heat to 375°F (190°C) on a deep-frying thermometer. Meanwhile, add all diced vegetables to batter and mix well.

Working in batches of about seven pakoras, carefully drop 1 heaping tablespoon of mixture for each pakora into hot oil. Cook, turning as necessary, until light golden brown, 1–2 minutes per side. Use a slotted spoon to remove pakoras to paper towels to drain. Repeat with remaining batter.

Just before serving pakoras, refry them in batches of seven, turning once, until crisp and golden brown, 1–2 minutes. Drain on paper towels. Serve immediately with raita.

NOTE You can do the initial frying of pakoras up to 6 hours ahead.

Paruppu vadai
Split-chickpea patties

Makes about 22 patties

1½ cups (10 oz/300 g) split chickpeas
   (garbanzo beans)
1 yellow (brown) onion, chopped
¼ bunch cilantro (fresh coriander),
   leaves and stems chopped
2 teaspoons crushed fresh ginger
2 teaspoons crushed garlic

2 fresh green chili peppers, finely
   chopped
4 teaspoons fennel seeds
1½ teaspoons cumin seeds
18 fresh curry leaves, finely chopped
salt to taste
vegetable oil, for deep-frying
Cucumber Raita (page 55) for serving

Place chickpeas in a bowl, add hot water to cover and soak for 2 hours. Drain
and reserve 1 cup (8 fl oz/250 ml) of soaking water.

Place chickpeas in a food processor and process until finely crushed, adding
1–2 tablespoons soaking water if necessary to make a smooth, thick paste. Add
onion, cilantro, ginger, garlic, chili peppers, fennel, cumin, curry leaves and salt,
and process until well chopped and combined.

Shape 2 tablespoons of chickpea mixture into a small patty and place on
a baking sheet. Repeat with remaining mixture.

Fill a karhai or wok with vegetable oil to a depth of 3 inches (7.5 cm). Heat
oil over medium–high heat to 375°F (190°C) on a deep-frying thermometer.
Cook patties in hot oil in batches of six, turning occasionally, until light golden
brown, 1–2 minutes. Use a slotted spoon to remove patties to paper towels
to drain.

Just before serving patties, refry in batches in hot oil until golden brown,
1–2 minutes. Drain on paper towels. Serve immediately with raita.

NOTE A karhai is a heavy bowl-shaped metal pan, similar to a wok, with handles
on either side. Karhai are available in Indian markets and some kitchenware
stores.

You can do the initial frying of patties up to 6 hours ahead.

Chicken

Chili chicken

Serves 8–10

1 cinnamon stick, about 3 inches (8 cm) long

2 teaspoons green cardamom pods

2 teaspoons whole cloves

1 teaspoon black peppercorns

1/3 cup (3/4 oz/20 g) chopped cilantro (fresh coriander)

36 fresh curry leaves

juice of 1 lemon

4 teaspoons finely chopped fresh green chili peppers

4 teaspoons finely grated fresh ginger

4 teaspoons crushed garlic

2 teaspoons tamarind concentrate

1 teaspoon ground turmeric

salt to taste

2 lb (1 kg) chicken thigh fillets, quartered

2 tablespoons vegetable oil

Preheat oven to 475°F (240°C/Gas 9).

In a spice grinder, grind cinnamon, cardamom, cloves and peppercorns to a powder. Transfer spices to a food processor and add cilantro, curry leaves, lemon juice, chili pepper, ginger, garlic, tamarind, turmeric and salt. Process to form a paste.

Place chicken pieces in a glass or ceramic bowl and add spice mixture. Mix well to coat chicken and set aside to marinate for 10–15 minutes.

Brush vegetable oil over a large baking sheet and spread coated chicken on sheet in a single layer. Bake, without turning, until chicken is cooked through, about 20 minutes. Serve immediately.

NOTE Serve the chicken with a salad made from 1 diced onion and 2 diced spring onions.

Dum ka murgh

Braised chicken

Serves 8–10

2 cups (1 lb/500 g) plain (natural)
   whole-milk yogurt

1 teaspoon crushed fresh ginger

1 teaspoon crushed garlic

½ teaspoon ground turmeric

1½ tablespoons sesame seeds, ground

8 blanched almonds, ground

salt to taste

2 lb (1 kg) chicken thigh fillets, halved
   or quartered (as desired)

1 cinnamon stick, about 1 inch (2.5 cm)
   long, broken into small pieces

2 green cardamom pods

4 whole cloves

½ teaspoon black cumin seeds

½ cup (4 fl oz/125 ml) vegetable oil
   and melted unsalted butter combined

3 yellow (brown) onions, thinly sliced

juice of 2 lemons

Steamed Basmati Rice (page 50) for
   serving

In a glass or ceramic bowl, combine
yogurt, ginger, garlic, turmeric,
sesame seeds, almonds and salt.

Add chicken and mix well. Cover
and marinate in the refrigerator for
1½ hours.

In a spice grinder, grind cinnamon,
cardamom, cloves and cumin to
a powder. Set aside.

In a large, heavy saucepan, heat oil
and butter mixture over medium heat.
Add onions and cook, uncovered,
stirring often, until dark golden
brown, about 15 minutes. Stir in
marinated chicken and mix well. Reduce heat to medium–low and cook,
uncovered, turning chicken and stirring sauce occasionally, until chicken is
cooked through, 20–25 minutes.

Stir in ground spices and lemon juice, and mix well. Simmer for 2 minutes.
Serve with rice.

Galinha cafreal
Chicken with green masala

Serves 8–10

1 bunch cilantro (fresh coriander),
leaves and stems coarsely chopped
¼ cup firmly packed fresh mint leaves
5 fresh green chili peppers, coarsely
chopped
4 teaspoons crushed fresh ginger
4 teaspoons crushed garlic

1 teaspoon coarsely ground black
peppercorns
salt to taste
juice of 1 lemon
1½ lb (750 g) chicken thigh fillets,
halved
4 teaspoons vegetable oil

Preheat oven to 475°F (240°C/
Gas 9).

Place cilantro, mint, chili pepper,
ginger, garlic, peppercorns and salt
in a food processor. Process to form
a thick paste, adding enough lemon
juice to moisten ingredients.

In a glass or ceramic bowl,
combine paste with chicken. Mix well
to coat chicken and set aside to
marinate for 20 minutes.

Brush vegetable oil over a large
baking sheet. Place chicken on sheet
in a single layer. Bake, without
turning, until chicken is cooked
through, 20–25 minutes.

Butter chicken

Serves 10

2 lb (1 kg) chicken thigh fillets

¼ cup (2 fl oz/60 ml) white vinegar
   or lemon juice

⅓ cup coriander seeds

1 cinnamon stick, about 2 inches
   (5 cm) long, broken into small
   pieces

5 brown or black cardamom pods

10 green cardamom pods

1 teaspoon whole cloves

3 teaspoons ground turmeric

2 teaspoons chili powder

2 teaspoons paprika

1 teaspoon ground nutmeg

1 teaspoon ground mace

¼ cup (2 oz/60 g) plain (natural)
   whole-milk yogurt

2½ tablespoons crushed garlic

2½ tablespoons grated fresh ginger

2½ tablespoons vegetable oil

salt to taste

SAUCE

½ cup (4 fl oz/125 ml) vegetable oil
   and melted unsalted butter combined

2 lb (1 kg) yellow (brown) onions, about
   6 medium, chopped

1 teaspoon salt, plus extra to taste

2½ tablespoons grated fresh ginger

2½ tablespoons crushed garlic

2 teaspoons chili powder

3 teaspoons ground turmeric

2 teaspoons chopped fresh green chili
   peppers

2 lb (1 kg) tomatoes, about 7 medium,
   chopped and pureed in a blender
   or food processor

⅔ cup (5 fl oz/150 ml) heavy (double)
   cream

¼ cup (2 oz/60 g) unsalted butter

4 teaspoons honey

2 tablespoons dried fenugreek leaves

⅓ cup (½ oz/15 g) chopped cilantro
   (fresh coriander)

Cut chicken fillets into quarters. In a glass or ceramic bowl, combine chicken with 4 teaspoons vinegar, and turn to coat. Set aside.

In a spice grinder, grind coriander seeds, cinnamon, cardamom and cloves to a powder. Place in a bowl and combine with turmeric, chili powder, paprika, nutmeg, mace, remaining vinegar, yogurt, garlic, ginger and oil, and mix well. Season with salt and add to chicken. Mix well, cover, and place in the refrigerator to marinate for 30 minutes.

Preheat oven to 475°F (240°C/Gas 9). Oil a shallow roasting pan and place chicken pieces in pan in a single layer. Bake, without turning, for 12 minutes.

Remove from oven and set aside.

To make sauce: In a deghchi or large frying pan, heat oil and butter mixture over medium–low heat. Add onions and 1 teaspoon salt and cook, uncovered, stirring occasionally, until onions are dark golden brown, 15–20 minutes. Add ginger and garlic and cook, stirring, for 2 minutes. Add chili powder, turmeric and chili pepper, and cook for 1 minute. Add tomatoes and cook, uncovered, stirring often, until tomatoes are soft, 5–10 minutes.

Add cream and butter to pan and cook, stirring, until butter melts. Stir in chicken, honey and fenugreek, and cook, stirring often, until chicken is cooked through, about 5 minutes. Stir in cilantro. Taste and add salt if necessary. Serve immediately.

Seafood

Meen kozhambu
Fish in coconut sauce

Serves 8

1 lb (500 g) white-fleshed fish fillets, such as snapper, barramundi or ocean perch

3 tablespoons vegetable oil

1 teaspoon brown or black mustard seeds

½ teaspoon fenugreek seeds

3 dried red chili peppers

1 lb (500 g) yellow (brown) onions, about 3 medium, halved and thinly sliced

2 tablespoons grated fresh ginger

2 tablespoons crushed garlic

36 fresh curry leaves

3 teaspoons ground turmeric

2–4 tablespoons chili powder

2 tomatoes, unpeeled, coarsely chopped

1½ cups (12 fl oz/375 ml) coconut cream

1 teaspoon tamarind concentrate

salt to taste

juice of ½ lemon

Steamed Basmati Rice (page 50), for serving

Remove skin from fish fillets then cut into ¾ x 2 inch (2 x 5 cm) pieces. Set aside.

In a karhai or wok, heat oil over low heat. Add mustard seeds and cook until seeds crackle, about 30 seconds. Add fenugreek seeds and chili peppers and cook, stirring, until seeds turn light golden brown and chili peppers are deep golden brown, about 30 seconds. Add onions and cook, stirring, until slightly softened, about 1 minute. Add ginger and garlic and cook, stirring, for 1 minute. Add curry leaves, turmeric and chili powder and cook, stirring, for 30 seconds. Add tomatoes and cook until tomatoes are slightly soft, about 3 minutes. Stir in coconut cream and tamarind, and season with salt.

Stir in fish pieces and simmer, covered, until fish is just cooked through, about 5 minutes. Stir in lemon juice. Serve immediately with rice.

Shrimp reiachado
Portuguese-style shrimp

Serves 8–10
1 recipe Reiachado Masala (page 16)
2 lb (1 kg) medium shrimp (prawns), peeled and deveined
2 tablespoons vegetable oil
juice of 1 lemon

In a glass or ceramic bowl, combine reiachado masala and shrimp and mix well to coat shrimp. Set aside to marinate for 5 minutes.

In a frying pan, heat oil over medium–low heat until hot. Cook shrimp in batches, turning once, until browned, about 1–2 minutes. Take care not to scorch marinade.

Drizzle cooked shrimp with lemon juice and serve hot.

VARIATION Lightly brush shrimp with reiachado masala. Cook shrimp in batches as above and set aside.

In a small saucepan, heat 2 tablespoons vegetable oil over medium–high heat. Cook 20 curry leaves—or as many as desired—until fragrant, about 30 seconds. Drain on paper towels and toss with shrimp. If desired, add thinly sliced red onion for color.

Goan fish

Serves 8–10

1–1½ cups dried red chili peppers,
   broken into small pieces
⅓ cup coriander seeds
¼ cup cumin seeds
¾ cup (6 fl oz/180 ml) white vinegar
1 tablespoon finely grated fresh ginger
1 tablespoon crushed garlic
2 teaspoons ground turmeric
½ cup (4 fl oz/125 ml) vegetable oil
   and melted unsalted butter combined

1 lb (500 g) yellow (brown) onions,
   about 3 medium, halved and sliced
2 large tomatoes, unpeeled, quartered
2 fresh green chili peppers, slit
   lengthwise
2½ cups (20 fl oz/625 ml) coconut milk
salt to taste
2 lb (1 kg) white-fleshed fish fillets
   such as snapper, ling, cod or ocean
   perch
Steamed Basmati Rice (page 50) for
   serving

In a spice grinder, grind dried chili pepper, coriander seeds and cumin seeds
to a powder. Place in a bowl and combine with vinegar, ginger, garlic and
turmeric to form a paste. Set aside.

In a large karhai or wok, heat oil and butter mixture over medium–low heat.
Add onions and cook, uncovered, stirring often, until soft, about 10 minutes.
Add spice paste and cook, stirring, until fragrant, about 3 minutes. Add
tomatoes, green chili peppers and coconut milk and cook, uncovered, stirring
often, until tomatoes soften, about
5 minutes. Season with salt.

If fish fillets are large, cut into
serving-sized pieces. Add fish to
sauce and cook, uncovered, until fish
flakes when tested with a fork, about
5 minutes. Serve hot with steamed
rice.

NOTE Adjust dried chili pepper
according to your taste—the full
quantity makes a hot dish.

Patra ni machchi
Fish steamed in banana leaves

Serves 10

peeled flesh from 1 fresh coconut (about 12 oz/375 g), coarsely chopped

6 fresh green chili peppers, coarsely chopped

2/3 cup (1 oz/30 g) chopped cilantro (fresh coriander)

1/2 cup (3/4 oz/20 g) chopped fresh mint

1/4 cup (2 fl oz/60 ml) vegetable oil

2 teaspoons crushed garlic

1/2 teaspoon ground turmeric

1 teaspoon cumin seeds

juice of 2 limes

1/4 teaspoon sugar

salt to taste

5 fresh banana leaves, center veins removed

2 lb (1 kg) large, white-fleshed fish fillets such as barramundi, ocean perch or snapper, cut into 10 serving-sized portions

lime wedges, for serving

Place coconut, chili pepper, cilantro, mint, oil, garlic, turmeric, cumin seeds, lime juice, sugar and salt in a food processor and process until finely minced to make a coconut chutney. Divide evenly into 10 portions and set aside.

Slowly pass each banana leaf over a medium–high gas flame until leaf turns bright green. Alternatively, heat a heavy frying pan over medium–high heat, place leaf in pan and heat until leaf turns bright green. Let leaves cool and cut into pieces large enough to wrap a fish portion.

Place a fish piece on a banana leaf piece. Spread a portion of coconut chutney over the fish. Wrap leaf around fish and tie with kitchen twine to secure. Repeat with remaining fish pieces, banana leaves and coconut chutney. Place fish parcels in a large bamboo steamer over a large wok half-filled with boiling water. Steam until fish flakes when tested with a fork, 12–15 minutes. Serve hot with lime wedges.

NOTE Heating banana leaves makes them malleable and easy to fold. If banana leaves are unavailable, use parchment (baking) paper or aluminum foil.

Meat

Bife vindalho
Beef vindaloo

Serves 8–10

5 dried red chili peppers, broken into small pieces
1 teaspoon cumin seeds
1 tablespoon black peppercorns
1½ tablespoons finely grated fresh ginger
1½ tablespoons crushed garlic
½ teaspoon ground turmeric
¾ cup (6 fl oz/180 ml) vegetable oil and melted unsalted butter combined
1½ lb (750 g) yellow (brown) onions, about 4½ medium, finely chopped
1 teaspoon salt, plus extra to taste
2 lb (1 kg) beef chuck, excess fat removed, cut into 1½-inch (4-cm) pieces
about 4 cups (32 fl oz/1 L) water
4 fresh green chili peppers, slit lengthwise
½ cup (4 fl oz/125 ml) white vinegar
½ teaspoon tamarind concentrate
½ teaspoon sugar
Steamed Basmati Rice (page 50), for serving

In a spice grinder, grind dried chili pepper, cumin seeds and peppercorns to a powder. Place in a bowl and combine with ginger, garlic and turmeric. Set aside.

In a karhai or wok, heat oil and butter mixture over medium–low heat. Add onions and 1 teaspoon salt and cook, uncovered, stirring often, until onions are dark golden brown, 20–25 minutes. Raise heat to medium–high and add beef. Cook, turning beef pieces, for 5 minutes. Add spice mixture and cook, stirring, until fragrant, about 2 minutes.

Pour in enough water to cover beef. Add chili peppers and bring to a simmer. Cook over low heat, partially covered, stirring occasionally, until liquid is reduced by half, about 1 hour.

Stir in vinegar, tamarind and sugar. Taste and add salt if necessary. Cook, uncovered, until sauce reduces and thickens, about 30 minutes. Serve hot with steamed rice.

Lamb cutlets baffad

Serves 6–8

¼ cup (2 fl oz/60 ml) vegetable oil and melted unsalted butter combined

2 yellow (brown) onions, chopped

½ teaspoon salt

2 tablespoons finely grated fresh ginger

2 tablespoons crushed garlic

3 tablespoons Baffad Masala (page 14)

2 tomatoes, unpeeled, chopped

4 teaspoons white vinegar

2 lb (1 kg) lamb cutlets

juice of ½ lemon

6–8 Chappati (page 51)

In a heavy saucepan, heat oil and butter mixture over medium–low heat. Add onions and salt and cook, uncovered, stirring often, until onions are dark golden brown, 10–15 minutes. Add ginger, garlic and baffad masala, and cook, stirring, until fragrant, about 1 minute.

Add tomatoes and vinegar to pan, and mix well, adding 1–2 tablespoons water to moisten mixture if necessary. Add lamb cutlets and turn to coat with sauce. Reduce heat to low and cook, uncovered, stirring often and turning lamb, adding a tablespoon or two of water if sauce begins to dry, until lamb is cooked to your liking and sauce is thick, 15–20 minutes.

Squeeze lemon juice over lamb and serve hot with chappati.

Lamb roganjosh

Serves 8–10
2 lb (1 kg) lamb shoulder, diced
2 cups (1 lb/500 g) plain (natural)
  whole-milk yogurt, whisked
1 teaspoon salt, plus extra to taste
⅔ cup (5 fl oz/150 ml) vegetable oil
  and melted unsalted butter combined
1 cinnamon stick
20 green cardamom pods
5 brown or black cardamom pods
1 teaspoon whole cloves

2 lb (1 kg) yellow (brown) onions,
  about 6 medium, chopped
2 tablespoons finely grated fresh ginger
2 tablespoons crushed garlic
4 teaspoons chili powder
2 teaspoons ground turmeric
⅓ cup (½ oz/15 g) chopped cilantro
  (fresh coriander)
1½ teaspoons Garam Masala (page 16)
Steamed Basmati Rice (page 50), for
  serving

In a large bowl, combine lamb, yogurt and ½ teaspoon salt and mix well. Set aside for 10 minutes.

In a large karhai or frying pan, heat oil and butter mixture over medium heat. Add cinnamon, cardamom and cloves and cook, stirring, until fragrant, about 30 seconds. Add onions and ½ teaspoon salt and cook over medium–low heat, uncovered, stirring often, until onions are golden brown, 20–25 minutes.

Add ginger and garlic and cook, stirring, for 30 seconds. Drain away any excess oil and butter, leaving onions and spices in pan.

Add lamb and yogurt mixture, chili powder and turmeric to pan and mix well. Cook over low heat, covered, until lamb is tender, 45–60 minutes. Add cilantro and garam masala and mix well. Taste and add salt if necessary. Serve hot with steamed rice.

NOTE You can use goat meat in place of lamb.

Kachche gosht ki biryani
Lamb biryani

Serves 10–12

4 yellow (brown) onions, halved and
   thinly sliced
1 teaspoon salt, plus extra to taste
1 cup (8 fl oz/250 ml) vegetable oil and
   melted unsalted butter combined
1¼ cups (10 oz/300 g) plain (natural)
   whole-milk yogurt
1 cup (1½ oz/45 g) chopped cilantro
   (fresh coriander)
1 cup (1½ oz/45 g) chopped fresh mint
6 fresh green chili peppers, chopped
1½ tablespoons finely grated fresh
   ginger
1½ tablespoons crushed garlic
1½ tablespoons Garam Masala
   (page 16)

2 tablespoons chili powder
1½ tablespoons ground turmeric
2 lb (1 kg) boneless lamb shoulder,
   diced
pinch saffron threads soaked in
   2 tablespoons hot milk for 10 minutes
2 lb (1 kg) basmati rice, rinsed and
   soaked in cold water to cover for
   20 minutes
boiling water
juice of 1 lemon
Churri (page 54), for serving

CRUST
3 cups (15 oz /450 g) whole wheat
   (wholemeal) flour
about 1 cup (8 fl oz/250 ml) water

Preheat oven to 475°F (240°C/Gas 9). In a glass or ceramic bowl, combine
onions with 1 teaspoon salt. Set aside for 10 minutes.

In a large deghchi or large, deep ovenproof saucepan, heat oil and butter
mixture over medium–low heat. Add onions and cook, uncovered, stirring often,
until onions are dark golden brown, 20–25 minutes. Strain onions and reserve
oil and butter mixture. Let onions cool slightly.

While onions are cooking, prepare crust. Place flour in a bowl and add enough
water to form a soft dough. Knead gently in bowl until smooth. Cover and set aside.

In a large glass or ceramic bowl, combine yogurt, cilantro, mint, chili pepper,
ginger, garlic, garam masala, chili powder and turmeric. Season with salt. Add
cooked onions, lamb, and saffron mixture and mix well. Spread lamb mixture
in base of deghchi or saucepan.

Drain rice and place in a large saucepan with enough boiling water to cover. Season with salt. Bring to a boil over high heat and cook, uncovered, for 7 minutes. Drain excess water from rice. Spread rice evenly over lamb mixture. Pour reserved oil and butter mixture evenly over rice. Cover tightly with lid. Roll crust dough into a thin sausage shape, long enough to extend around top edge of deghchi or saucepan. Place dough around edge, molding it to seal lid.

Place deghchi or saucepan over medium–high heat for 5 minutes, then transfer to oven. Reduce oven temperature to 400°F (200°C/Gas 6) and cook for 40 minutes. Remove from oven and let stand for 15 minutes before breaking away crust and removing lid. Either serve from pan or place a large platter over deghchi or saucepan and then very carefully invert biryani onto platter (you will need two people to do this). Serve immediately, drizzled with lemon juice and accompanied by churri.

NOTE A long piece of aluminum foil can be used, "scrunched" around top edge of deghchi or saucepan, to create a seal (in place of crust).

Vegetarian Dishes

Moong matar dhaniwal
Creamy lentil and split-pea dal

Serves 6–8

⅔ cup (5 oz/150 g) lentils, rinsed and drained
⅔ cup (5 oz/150 g) yellow split peas, rinsed and drained
1 teaspoon ground turmeric
2 fresh green chili peppers, halved lengthwise
4 teaspoons vegetable oil
1 teaspoon brown or black mustard seeds
1 teaspoon cumin seeds
2 teaspoons Garam Masala (page 16)
1 teaspoon ground coriander
½ cup (4 fl oz/125 ml) water
3 tablespoons heavy (double) cream
1 large tomato, unpeeled, chopped
salt to taste
¼ cup (⅓ oz/10 g) chopped cilantro (fresh coriander)

Place lentils and split peas in a bowl and add cold water to cover. Set aside for 30 minutes. Drain.

Fill a large saucepan with water and bring to a boil. Add lentils, split peas, turmeric and chili pepper. Boil, uncovered, until lentils and peas are tender, about 30 minutes. Drain, place in a bowl and mash coarsely. Set aside.

In a saucepan, heat oil over medium–low heat and add mustard seeds. Cook until they crackle, about 30 seconds. Stir in cumin seeds and cook until aromatic, about 30 seconds. Stir in garam masala and coriander. Stir in mashed lentils and peas, water, cream and tomato. Season with salt. Bring to a boil over medium heat, reduce heat to low and simmer, partially covered, stirring often, for 4 minutes. Adjust seasoning. Stir in cilantro and serve hot.

Palak paneer
Homemade cottage cheese with spinach

Serves 10

PANEER

4 qt (4 L) whole (full cream) milk

1²⁄₃ cups (13 fl oz/400 ml) heavy (double) cream

²⁄₃ cup (5 fl oz/150 ml) white vinegar

2 bunches spinach, trimmed and rinsed well

1½ teaspoons ground turmeric

2 tablespoons water

3 tablespoons vegetable oil and melted unsalted butter combined

4 teaspoons cumin seeds

3 yellow (brown) onions, chopped

½ teaspoon salt

2 tablespoons coriander seeds, crushed

1½ tablespoons grated fresh ginger

2 fresh green chili peppers, finely chopped

1 teaspoon chili powder

3 tomatoes, unpeeled, finely chopped

1 teaspoon dried fenugreek leaves

Chappati (page 51) for serving

To make paneer: Line a large, flat-bottomed sieve with a double layer of cheesecloth (muslin), allowing it to overhang sides of sieve. Place lined sieve inside a large other bowl. Choose a large, heavy, non-aluminum saucepan that fits inside the sieve.

Pour milk into the saucepan and bring slowly to a boil over medium heat. When milk is almost boiling, stir in cream and bring to a boil again. When milk mixture just comes to a boil (it will begin to bubble and froth, and vibrations from boiling mixture can be felt in the handle of a metal spoon held in milk), pour in vinegar and remove from heat. Set aside for 2 minutes; do not stir.

Using a large slotted spoon or spoon-shaped strainer, gently lift curds from whey and place in lined sieve. Once all curds have been placed in sieve, carefully tie loose ends of cheesecloth together to form curds into a thick, round disk about 10 inches (25 cm) in diameter. Return whey in bowl back to saucepan holding remainder of whey. Place saucepan on top of paneer to weight it. Set aside at room temperature until paneer is firm, about 25 minutes. Remove saucepan from paneer. Carefully untie cheesecloth, remove paneer and cut into 1-inch (2.5-cm) pieces.

Place spinach in a large saucepan. In a small bowl, combine ½ teaspoon turmeric with water and add to pan. Cook over medium–high heat, covered, turning spinach occasionally, until spinach is wilted, 3–5 minutes. Remove from heat, drain excess water and let spinach cool. Place spinach in a food processor or blender and puree. Set aside.

In a karhai or wok, heat oil and butter mixture over medium–low heat. Add cumin seeds and cook until fragrant, about 30 seconds. Add onions and salt and cook uncovered, stirring often, until onions are translucent, about 5 minutes.

Add coriander seeds, ginger, chili pepper, chili powder and remaining 1 teaspoon turmeric and cook, stirring, until fragrant, 2–3 minutes.

Stir in tomatoes and cook, stirring occasionally, until tomatoes are soft, about 5 minutes. Stir in pureed spinach and mix well. Add paneer and stir gently to coat with sauce. Cook over medium–low heat until paneer is warmed through, 2–3 minutes. Sprinkle with fenugreek leaves and serve hot with chappati.

NOTE If not using paneer immediately, place flat in an airtight container and add enough whey to cover. Store in the refrigerator for up to 1 week.

Adding turmeric to spinach before cooking helps spinach retain a bright green color.

Masala dosai

Rice and lentil pancakes with potato filling

Makes 10–12 filled pancakes

FOR PANCAKES

3½ cups (16 oz/660 g) medium to
  coarse rice flour

1¼ cups (5 oz/150 g) split black lentil
  flour

salt as needed

cold water as needed

½ cup (4 fl oz/125 ml) vegetable oil
  and melted unsalted butter combined

FOR FILLING

2 tablespoons vegetable oil

1½ teaspoons brown or black mustard
  seeds

1 tablespoon split chickpeas (garbanzo
  beans)

1 tablespoon split black lentils

4 dried red chili peppers

¼ teaspoon powdered asafoetida

2½ teaspoons ground turmeric

18 fresh curry leaves

2 yellow (brown) onions, halved and
  thinly sliced

½ teaspoon salt, plus extra salt to taste

2 lb (1 kg) cooked desiree or pontiac
  potatoes, (about 7 medium), peeled
  and coarsely mashed

½ cup (1 oz/30 g) chopped cilantro
  (fresh coriander)

Sambhar (see page 54) and Fresh
  Coconut Chutney (page 53), for
  serving

To make pancakes: In a bowl, combine ⅓ cup (2 oz/60 g) rice flour with
2 tablespoons (⅔ oz/20 g) lentil flour and a pinch of salt. Make a well in center.
Stir in enough cold water to form a batter with a dropping consistency. Cover
and let stand in a warm place for 12 hours or overnight.

In a clean bowl, combine ⅓ cup (2 oz/60 g) rice flour with 2 tablespoons
(⅔ oz/20 g) lentil flour and a pinch salt. Make a well in center. Stir in enough
cold water to form a batter with a dropping consistency. Stir 1 heaping
tablespoon of previous day's batter into new batter. Discard remainder of old
batter. Cover new batter and let stand in a warm place for 12 hours or overnight.

In a large clean bowl, combine remaining rice flour with remaining lentil flour
and 1 teaspoon salt. Stir in enough cold water to form a new batter with a soft
dropping consistency. Stir 1 heaping tablespoon of previous day's batter into
new batter. Discard old batter. Cover new batter and let stand in a warm place

for 12 hours or overnight. By this stage, the batter should have increased in volume by about half.

To cook pancakes: Heat a heavy flat griddle over high heat. Use a flat-bottomed metal cup to ladle ⅓ cup (2½ fl oz/80 ml) batter at a time onto pan. Use bottom of cup to spread batter outwards, moving cup in concentric circles. Each pancake should be 7–8 inches (18–20 cm) in diameter.

Drizzle pancake with 1 teaspoon oil and butter mixture and cook until crisp and golden underneath, 2–4 minutes. Place filling along center and roll or fold as desired. Place, seam-side down, on a plate. Repeat with remaining batter and oil and butter mixture.

To make filling: In a heavy saucepan, heat oil over medium–low heat. Add mustard seeds and cook until they crackle, about 30 seconds. Add chickpeas and lentils and cook over low heat, stirring, until light golden, about 30 seconds; be careful not to burn them. Add chili peppers and asafoetida and cook, stirring, for 15 seconds. Add turmeric and curry leaves and cook, stirring, for 15 seconds. Stir in onions and ½ teaspoon salt and cook, stirring often, until onions are translucent, about 5 minutes. Add potatoes and cilantro and cook,

stirring, until well combined, 2–3 minutes. Taste and adjust seasoning if necessary. Cover to keep warm and set aside until serving.

Spoon one-tenth of potato filling onto each dosai, fold in sides and place on a serving plate, seam-side down. Serve immediately with sambhar and chutney.

NOTE You will need to cook pancakes just before serving, but filling can be made 6 hours ahead.

Jeera aloo

Cumin-flavored potatoes

Serves 8–10

2 lb (1 kg) uniformly sized desiree or pontiac potatoes, about 7 medium

salt as needed

2½ tablespoons cold water

1 teaspoon ground turmeric

½ teaspoon chili powder

¼ cup (2 fl oz/60 ml) vegetable oil and melted unsalted butter combined

4 teaspoons cumin seeds

4 teaspoons ground coriander

2 teaspoons finely grated fresh ginger

⅓ cup (½ oz/15 g) chopped cilantro (fresh coriander)

juice of ½ lemon

Place potatoes and large pinch salt in a saucepan with enough cold water to cover. Bring to a boil over medium–high heat. Reduce heat to medium–low and cook, partially covered, until potatoes are tender, about 20 minutes. Drain potatoes and let cool for 15 minutes. Peel potatoes and cut into 1½-inch (4-cm) cubes. Set aside.

In a small bowl, combine cold water, turmeric and chili powder; set aside.

In a large, heavy saucepan, heat oil and butter mixture over medium–low heat. Add cumin seeds and cook, stirring, until fragrant, about 30 seconds; take care not to burn seeds. Reduce heat to low and add water and turmeric mixture. Cook, stirring, for 30 seconds. Add potatoes and salt to taste, and toss gently until heated through, about 1 minute. Add coriander and toss for 30 seconds. Add ginger and cilantro and toss to combine. Drizzle with lemon juice and serve.

Vegetable pulao

Serves 8

2½ cups (1 lb/500 g) basmati rice

⅓ cup (3 fl oz/90 ml) vegetable oil and melted unsalted butter combined

¾-inch (2-cm) piece cinnamon stick

1 brown or black cardamom pod

2 green cardamom pods

2 whole cloves

½ mace blade

2 yellow (brown) onions, halved and thinly sliced

about 1 teaspoon salt

1 tablespoon finely grated fresh ginger

1 tablespoon crushed garlic

2 tomatoes, unpeeled, finely chopped

1 carrot, cut into 1-inch (2.5-cm) sticks

4 oz (125 g) green beans, trimmed and cut into 1-inch (2.5-cm) sticks

½ cup (2½ oz/75 g) shelled fresh or frozen green peas

1½ tablespoons chopped fresh green chili peppers

3¾ cups (30 fl oz/940 ml) vegetable stock or water

½ cup (¾ oz/25 g) chopped cilantro (fresh coriander), for serving

Place rice in a bowl and add cold water to cover. Swirl rice with your hand, let rice settle, then drain off water. Repeat six or seven times. Cover rice with water and set aside to soak for 20 minutes.

Preheat oven to 350°F (180°C/Gas 4). In a large, heavy deghchi or ovenproof saucepan, heat oil and butter mixture over low heat. Add cinnamon, cardamom, cloves and mace and cook, stirring, until fragrant, about 30 seconds. Add onions and salt and cook, uncovered, stirring occasionally, until onions are dark golden brown, about 15 minutes.

Add ginger and garlic and cook for 30 seconds. Stir in tomatoes and mix well. Stir in carrot, beans, peas and chili pepper, and cook, stirring, for 3 minutes.

Drain rice and add to pan, stirring until well combined. Stir in stock and bring to a simmer. Cook, partially covered, until tunnels begin to appear in rice mixture, about 10 minutes.

Cover pan tightly and bake in oven until rice is tender, about 15 minutes. Remove from oven and let stand for 10 minutes. Garnish with cilantro and serve immediately.

Accompaniments

Steamed basmati rice

Serves 8–10
2½ cups (1 lb/500 g) basmati rice
5 cups (40 fl oz/1.2 L) water
½ teaspoon salt

Place rice in a bowl and add cold water to cover. Swirl with your hand, let rice settle, then drain off water. Repeat six or seven times. Add 5 cups (40 fl oz/1.2 L) water to rice and set aside to soak for 20 minutes.

Drain water from rice into a large, heavy saucepan with a tight-fitting lid. Add salt and bring to a boil over medium–high heat. Add soaked rice,

stir once, then bring to a boil. Reduce heat to low and cook, partially covered, until most of the water is absorbed and steam holes appear in the rice, 10–15 minutes.

Cover and reduce heat to very low. Let rice steam for 10 minutes without lifting lid. Remove from heat and set aside for 5–10 minutes without lifting lid. Fluff grains with a fork and serve.

NOTE Used throughout India, basmati rice has a delightfully unique fragrance when cooked, and complements all Indian food. Once cooked, the rice grains should not stick together but should be separate grains. Rinse rice well before cooking to remove excess starch; otherwise rice can become gluey. A general guide is to soak rice in twice its volume of water then cook it in soaking water. The rice must be steamed over very low heat for last 10 minutes of cooking. Use a heat diffuser if you have one, or place saucepan on a wok stand over heat source.

Chappati
Flat bread

Makes 12 chappati
5 cups (1½ lb/750 g) whole wheat (wholemeal) flour
1 teaspoon salt
3 tablespoons vegetable oil
about 2 cups (16 fl oz/500 ml) water
vegetable oil and melted unsalted butter combined, for brushing

Sift flour and salt into a large mixing bowl. Make a well in center. Add oil and enough water, adding water in increments, to form a soft dough with your hand. Knead dough lightly in bowl, cover with a clean damp kitchen towel, and set aside for 20 minutes.

Turn out dough onto a lightly floured surface and knead until it almost springs back when touched lightly, about 10 minutes. Cover with a damp towel and set aside for 15 minutes. Knead dough lightly and divide evenly into 12 portions. Shape each portion into a ball, then roll out into a disk 8–10 inches (20–25 cm) in diameter.

Heat a heavy cast-iron griddle over medium heat. When griddle is hot, place a disk of dough on griddle and cook, lightly pressing disk all over with a dry clean kitchen towel, using a dabbing motion, until disk is golden brown in spots, 1–2 minutes. Turn and cook on second side until golden brown in spots and cooked through, about 1 minute. Brush with oil and butter mixture and remove to a serving tray lined with a cloth napkin. Repeat with remaining disks.

NOTE The griddle must not be too hot or chappati will become dry and burnt. You can also make chappati smaller if you prefer. Chappati can be cooked several hours ahead. Before serving, wrap them in a clean kitchen towel, then aluminum foil, and heat in an oven preheated to 225°F (110°C/Gas ¼) for 5–10 minutes.

Date and tamarind chutney

Makes about 6 cups (48 fl oz/1.5 L)
2 lb (1 kg) pitted, dried dates
3 cups (24 fl oz/750 ml) white vinegar
8 oz (250 g) jaggery or dark brown
  sugar
¾ cup (6 oz/180 g) salt
1 cup (8 fl oz/250 ml) vegetable oil

⅓ cup (3½ oz/105 g) tamarind
  concentrate
⅔ cup (3 oz/90 g) chili powder
5 x 3-inch (7.5-cm) cinnamon sticks,
  broken into 1-inch (2.5-cm) pieces
2½ tablespoons green cardamom pods
3 tablespoons whole cloves
4 teaspoons chat masala

In a large, heavy saucepan, combine dates, vinegar, jaggery, salt, oil, tamarind, chili powder, cinnamon, cardamom and cloves. Cook over medium heat, stirring, until mixture begins to bubble. Reduce heat to low and cook, partially covered and stirring often, until dates are soft, 35–45 minutes.

Remove from heat, add chat masala and mix well. Spoon hot chutney into clean glass jars and immediately seal with lids. Turn jars upside-down and set aside for 5 minutes. Turn upright and set aside to cool. Label with name and date. Store in a cool cupboard for at least 1 week before opening.

NOTE Unopened chutney will keep for up to 1 year in a cool, dark cupboard. After opening, it will keep in the refrigerator for up to 6 months. The chutney sterilizes the jars and lids because the jars are filled, sealed and inverted while the chutney is boiling hot.

Fresh coconut chutney

Serves 8

peeled flesh from 1 fresh coconut
(about 12 oz/375 g), coarsely
chopped

½ cup (¾ oz/20 g) coarsely chopped
cilantro (fresh coriander) leaves and
stems

2 fresh green chili peppers, coarsely
chopped

2½ teaspoons finely grated fresh ginger

salt to taste

3–4 tablespoons cold water

2 teaspoons vegetable oil

1½ teaspoons brown or black mustard
seeds

½ teaspoon powdered asafoetida

18 fresh curry leaves, coarsely chopped

Place coconut in a food processor and
process until finely chopped. Add
cilantro, chili pepper, ginger and salt.
Process until all ingredients are finely
chopped, adding 3–4 tablespoons
water if necessary to facilitate
processing. Transfer mixture to a bowl.

In a small saucepan, heat oil over
medium heat. Add mustard seeds and
cook, stirring, until they begin to
crackle, about 30 seconds. Remove
from heat and quickly stir in
asafoetida and curry leaves, mixing
well.

Add mustard seed mixture to
coconut chutney and mix well. Taste
and add salt if necessary.

NOTE Chutney can be made 1 day
ahead. Store in an airtight container
in the refrigerator.

Sambhar
Lentil gravy

Serves 10-12

1½ cups (10 oz/300 g) split yellow
   lentils, rinsed and drained
8 cups (64 fl oz/2 L) water
1 teaspoon ground turmeric
1 lb (500 g) tomatoes, about
   3–4 medium, unpeeled, chopped
2 yellow (brown) onions, chopped
3 tablespoons Sambhar Masala
   (page 14)
2 teaspoons tamarind concentrate
18 fresh curry leaves
salt to taste
⅔ cup (1 oz/30 g) chopped cilantro
   (fresh coriander)

In a large saucepan, combine lentils,
water and turmeric, and bring to a
boil. Reduce heat to low and cook,
partially covered, until lentils are soft
and mushy, about 30 minutes.

Add tomatoes and onions and cook,
partially covered, stirring occasionally,
until soft, about 30 minutes. Add
sambhar masala, tamarind, curry
leaves and salt, and bring to a boil.

Taste and adjust seasoning. Stir in
cilantro. Partially cover and keep
warm over low heat until serving.

Churri
Herb and ginger yogurt dip

Serves 8–10

1 teaspoon cumin seeds
½ cup (¾ oz/20 g) coarsely chopped
   fresh mint
½ cup (¾ oz/20 g) coarsely chopped
   cilantro (fresh coriander)
2 teaspoons finely chopped fresh ginger
2 fresh green chili peppers, coarsely
   chopped
2½ cups (20 oz/600 g) plain (natural)
   whole-milk yogurt
1 yellow (brown) onion, halved and
   thinly sliced
salt to taste

In a small saucepan over low heat,
dry-roast cumin seeds until fragrant
and lightly colored, being careful not
to burn them. Let cool, then grind
to a powder in a spice grinder.

Place mint, cilantro, ginger and
chili pepper in a food processor and
process until finely chopped.

In a bowl, whisk yogurt. Add onion,
ground cumin and chopped herb
mixture. Mix well and season with salt.

NOTE Churri can be made 2 days
ahead. Store in an airtight container
in the refrigerator.

Cucumber raita

Cucumber and yogurt dip

Serves 8

1 ½ teaspoons cumin seeds
1 cup (8 oz/250 g) plain (natural) whole-milk yogurt
1 English (hothouse) cucumber, finely chopped
salt and freshly ground black pepper to taste
¼ cup (⅓ oz/10 g) chopped cilantro (fresh coriander)

In a small saucepan over low heat, dry-roast cumin seeds until fragrant and lightly colored, being careful not to burn them. Let cool, then grind to a powder in a spice grinder.

In a bowl, whisk yogurt. Add cucumber and ground cumin, and season with salt and pepper. Mix well. Stir in cilantro and mix well.

NOTE This raita can be made up to 6 hours ahead. Store in an airtight container in the refrigerator.

Desserts and Drinks

Pista kulfi
Pistachio ice cream

Serves 10

large pinch saffron threads (optional)
½ cup (4 fl oz/125 ml) milk, heated
⅓ cup (3½ oz/105 g) pistachio nuts
3 tablespoons green cardamom pods
1⅔ cups (13 fl oz/400 ml) sweetened
  condensed milk
3 cups (24 fl oz/750 ml) heavy (double)
  cream

RICH SAUCE
½ cup (4 oz/125 g) raw or Demerara
  sugar
½ cup (4 fl oz/125 ml) heavy (double)
  cream
5 star anise

If using saffron, place in a bowl with hot milk and set aside for 10 minutes. Place pistachio nuts in a food processor and process until finely chopped. In a spice grinder, grind cardamom to a powder.

Place condensed milk and cream in a bowl. Stir until well combined; do not whisk or beat. Add pistachio nuts, milk mixture and ground cardamom. Stir until well combined. Divide mixture among 10 ramekins with a ½-cup (4-fl oz/125-ml) capacity. Place in freezer until ice cream is frozen, about 6 hours. Cover ramekins well and keep in freezer until serving.

To make sauce: In a saucepan, combine sugar, cream and star anise. Stir over low heat until sugar dissolves. Bring to a boil, reduce heat to low and cook, uncovered, stirring often, until slightly thickened, about 10 minutes.

To serve, briefly dip each ramekin in a bowl of hot water. Invert a serving plate on top and invert plate and ramekin to unmold ice cream. Top with sauce and serve immediately.

NOTE You can make ice cream up to 2 weeks ahead. Wrap well to prevent flavors from other foods in freezer being absorbed. Make sauce close to serving.

Gajar ka halwa
Carrot and cardamom milk pudding

Serves 10

2 lb (1 kg) carrots, about 9 medium, peeled and grated

8 cups (64 fl oz/2 L) whole (full cream) milk

3 tablespoons green cardamom pods

6–8 saffron threads

½ cup (4 fl oz/125 ml) whole (full cream) milk, heated

½ cup (2 oz/60 g) sliced (flaked) almonds

½ cup (2 oz/60 g) pistachio nuts, sliced

1 cup (8 oz/250 g) sugar

⅓ cup (2 oz/60 g) raisins

⅔ cup (5 oz/150 g) ghee or unsalted butter

Preheat oven to 350°F (180°C/Gas 4).

In a large, heavy saucepan, combine carrots and 8 cups (64 fl oz/2 L) milk and bring to a boil over medium–high heat. Reduce heat to medium and cook, uncovered, stirring often, until most of milk is absorbed and carrots are soft, about 1¼ hours.

While carrots are cooking, grind cardamom to a powder in a spice grinder. Set aside.

In a bowl, combine saffron and hot milk; set aside for 10 minutes.

Spread almonds and pistachios on a baking sheet and toast in oven, stirring nuts occasionally, for 6–8 minutes. Remove from oven and let cool.

Add cardamom, saffron mixture, sugar and raisins to carrot mixture and cook, stirring, until sugar dissolves. Simmer, uncovered, stirring often, until all liquid is absorbed, about 45 minutes.

Add ghee or butter, a spoonful at a time, stirring until combined. Cook, stirring often, until pudding begins to pull away from sides of pan, 10–15 minutes. Stir in three-fourths of nuts. Spoon into bowls and sprinkle with remaining nuts. Serve warm.

NOTE You can spread pudding evenly in a shallow 8-inch (20-cm) square baking pan lined with plastic wrap. Refrigerate until cold. Use plastic wrap to lift pudding from pan. Cut pudding into individual portions to serve.

Lassi
Chilled yogurt drink

Serves 10

pinch saffron threads
⅔ cup (5 fl oz/150 ml) milk, heated
3 tablespoons green cardamom pods
8 cups (4 lb/2 kg) plain (natural) whole-milk yogurt
½ cup (3½ oz/105 g) superfine (caster) sugar
crushed ice, for serving

In a bowl, combine saffron and warm milk; set aside for 10 minutes.

In a spice grinder, grind cardamom to a powder.

In a large bowl, combine saffron mixture, cardamom, yogurt and sugar. Whisk thoroughly until sugar dissolves and mixture begins to froth.

Pour into glasses, add crushed ice and serve immediately.

NOTE You can thin lassi by adding milk.

Meera's masala chai
Meera's Indian tea

Serves 8
4 cups (32 fl oz/1 L) cold water
4 teaspoons finely grated fresh ginger
⅓ cup (1 oz/30 g) tea leaves
3 tablespoons milk, plus extra for serving
½ teaspoon Garam Masala (page 16)
sugar to taste

In a saucepan, combine water and ginger and bring to a boil over medium heat. Reduce heat and stir in tea leaves. Bring to a boil again and stir in 3 tablespoons milk and garam masala.

Remove from heat and cover pan. Set aside for 4 minutes. Strain and add sugar to taste. Serve with extra milk.

NOTE: Indians generally drink their chai strong with lots of milk and sugar, but you can vary the amounts depending on how strong or diluted you like your chai. As a variation, use ground cardamom instead of garam masala.

Index

INDEX

A LANSDOWNE BOOK

Published by Apple Press
Sheridan House
4th Floor
112-116 Western Road
Hove
East Sussex BN3 1DD UK

www.apple-press.com

Created and produced by Lansdowne Publishing
Text: Jan Purser and Ajoy Joshi
Photographer: Alan Benson
Stylist: Marie-Helene Clauzon
Food Preparation: Rodney Dunn
Designer: Avril Makula
Production: Sally Stokes and Eleanor Cant
Project Co-ordinator: Sally Hurworth

ISBN 1 84543 077 8

Set in Trade Gothic, Journal Text, Gill Sans and Neuropol on QuarkXPress
Printed in Singapore by Tien Wah Press

Cover picture: Jeera aloo (Cumin-flavored potatoes), page 46
Pictured on page 2: Fresh coconut chutney, page 53
Pictured on page 4: Chili chicken, page 22